D0517612

PHOTOGRAPHS ✦ CHRIS REARDON

LOUISBOURG

THE PHOENIX FORTRESS

TEXT ✦ A.J.B. JOHNSTON

To Louisbourg and to the profound sense of living history that it inspires.

Copyright © Chris Reardon and A.J.B. Johnston, 1990

All rights reserved. No part of this work covered by the copyrights hereon may be reproduced or used in any form or by any means—graphic, electronic, or mechanical—without the prior written permission of the publisher. Any request for photocopying, recording, taping, or information storage and retrieval systems of any part of this book shall be directed in writing to the Canadian Reprography Collective, 379 Adelaide Street West, Suite M1, Toronto, Ontario, M5V 1S5.

Nimbus Publishing Limited
P.O. Box 9301, Station A
Halifax, Nova Scotia
B3K 5N5

Design: Steven Slipp, GDA, Halifax
Printing and binding: Everbest Printing Co., Ltd., Hong Kong

Canadian Cataloguing in Publication Data
Reardon, Chris.
Louisbourg

ISBN 0-921054-35-1 PB
ISBN 0-921054-51-3 HC

1. Louisbourg (N.S.)—Description—Views.
I. Johnston, A. J. B. II. Title.

FC2349.L8R42 1990   971.6'955'0222   C90-097539-3
F1039.5.L8R42 1990

The authors would like to thank Don MacLennan and Andrée Crépeau of Sydney, Nova Scotia, for their continued support and enthusiasm. As well, they are grateful to Robert Pichette, also of Sydney, for his ongoing interest in the project.

CONTENTS

INTRODUCTION / 1

❖

SEAPORT / 12

❖

FORTRESS / 30

❖

COMMUNITY / 52

Sir, I am commanded by His Majesty to acquaint you, that ... the fortress at Louisbourg ... together with all the works and defences of the harbour, be most effectively, and most entirely, demolished....
—WILLIAM PITT, BRITISH PRIME MINISTER, 1760

What could be more stimulating to the imagination or instructive to the mind ... than to look upon a symbolic reconstruction of the Fortress of Louisbourg.
—I. C. RAND, CANADIAN ROYAL COMMISSIONER, 1960

INTRODUCTION

ON THE SOUTHEAST COAST OF CAPE BRETON, at the tip of a rugged landscape that juts out into the grey Atlantic, along a shore that has been punished by summer fogs and winter winds since time immemorial, stands one of the most intriguing phenomena of the twentieth century. There, exposed to the endless blasts of the sea, rise more than 50 eighteenth-century buildings. Nothing too unusual about that, you might say. There are a number of communities along the Atlantic seaboard that have colonial-era houses. In this case, however, not one of the eighteenth-century structures is yet thirty years old.

What you see is no chimera, though it is an illusion of sorts. It is a walled town that was and now is again. It is the Fortress of Louisbourg, a national historic park that the *Michelin Guide* rates as the finest attraction in Atlantic Canada.

What is this place, this Louisbourg, this faraway fortress that rises out of the Atlantic like a grey ghost? Is it what it seems to be, a shadow on the waters of time? A phoenix given its wing by some unforeseen fire of history?

It is that—and much more. For most people Louisbourg is a place to visit, a four- or five-hour walk through the past. It is one of the world's great outdoor museums, offering an unforgettable window on the summer of 1744. It pays homage to a time when mighty powers fought bitterly over possession of the New World. And it is an experiment, an attempt to do the impossible: the phoenix fortress recaptures the minutiae and the essence of a lost world.

In its original heyday Louisbourg was a leading player on the world stage: flourishing seaport, military stronghold, spirited community. The town grew and prospered for decades. Then, at its peak, barely a half-century old, it disappeared, a casualty of the Anglo-French struggle for North America.

How has Louisbourg come to stand again? The answer speaks of eighteenth-century wars and twentieth-century politics.

The France of the Sun King, Louis XIV, gave birth to Louisbourg, establishing it in 1713 as a fishing base-cum-strategic stronghold. The settlement came nearly two centuries after Jacques Cartier's first voyage to the New World and one century after Pierre du Gua de Monts

THE FRANCE OF THE SUN KING, LOUIS XIV, *gave birth to Louisbourg, establishing it in 1713 as a fishing base and strategic stronghold.*

and Samuel de Champlain established Port Royal, Nova Scotia. By the time of the founding of Louisbourg, France was no longer the only European power in what is now Atlantic Canada. Britain had successfully challenged France's territorial claims and rivalled it in exploiting the lucrative cod fishery. One war followed another as the imperial powers sought domination. With the signing of the peace treaty at Utrecht, Holland, in 1713, the French found themselves ousted from the region from all but two islands, Ile Royale (Cape Breton) and Ile Saint-Jean (Prince Edward Island). In that limited sphere the French determined to try again. Louisbourg became their new hope on the coastal frontier of New France.

Perfectly situated for the triangular trade routes between France and her New World colonies, Louisbourg emerged as one of the busiest ports in North America. More than one hundred vessels sailed into its sheltered harbor every year. Merchants from France, the West Indies, Québec, Acadia, and the American colonies came to do business. Import and export trade thrived. Ile Royale exported cod to Europe and the Antilles, and goods and products from far and wide—from Bordeaux wines to Chinese porcelain—came to Ile Royale.

With prosperity came growth. In 1713 Louisbourg's population comprised 116 men, 10 women, and 23 children; three decades later it reached about 2,000; by the 1750s it was approximately 4,000. Most people resided within the walls of the fortress, though the fishing population lived next to the sea. Their dwellings, wharves, and flakes ringed the harbor.

To protect the settlement, France's first port of call in the New World, the town was completely enclosed by fortifications. Military engineers designed those defences, which followed the basic precepts of the era, as perfected by the great Vauban during Louis XIV's reign. Although the fortress was nothing special when compared with elaborate European defences, Louisbourg did possess an *enceinte* that was massive by North American standards. The usual defences in the New World were earthworks or palisades; Ile Royale's capital had nearly two miles of perimeter walls, seven bastions, five guardhouses, four monumental gates, two outlying batteries, and more than one hundred cannons. In fact, Louisbourg became so vital to French interests during Louis XV's reign (1715–1774) that Voltaire called it "the key to their possessions in the North America."

Consequently, Louisbourg drew the envy and ire of its commercial rivals and territorial enemies. The British saw it as the guardian of the Gulf of St. Lawrence, as the bastioned rampart at the northern mouth of the continent. Twice the British attacked, and twice Louisbourg fell. Each time, the siege lasted from six to seven weeks. Each time, enemy forces had to carry out a naval blockade to shut off French supplies and reinforcements.

At the beginning of the first siege, a virtual crusade undertaken by New England amateurs in 1745, Benjamin Franklin warned his brother, among the besiegers, not to expect immediate success. "Fortified towns are hard nuts to crack," Franklin wrote, "and your teeth have not been accustomed to it." But Louisbourg did crack, and all New England rejoiced. It was America's first major military victory and, some historians have argued, a precursor to the war for independence waged a generation later.

The celebrations in New England were loud and long. The Americans were so proud of their conquest that when British diplomats handed Louisbourg back to the French in 1748, in the Treaty of Aix-la-Chapelle, New Englanders felt utterly betrayed—another cause of colonial alienation from Britain.

The French who had lived in Louisbourg before 1745 returned to their Ile Royale fishing base and fortress in 1749. For four years they had waited and worried in France, wondering whether they would ever see the island again. When diplomacy gave them back Louisbourg, most of them eagerly made the transatlantic crossing one more time. For several years their lives were once again ruled by cod catches and balance sheets, garrison routines and property disputes, baptisms and marriages. Then, in the mid-1750s, another Anglo-French war broke out. A dreaded assault threatened Louisbourg in 1757 and was finally launched in earnest in 1758. It was a contest of epic proportions. Twenty-seven thousand British soldiers and sailors blockaded and bombarded the town. Louisbourg fell a second time. The following year Québec capitulated. Then Montréal. Suddenly, after two centuries of conflict, New France became British America. Louisbourg's citizens were sent back to France; the more numerous St. Lawrence-valley French stayed on, becoming today's Québécois.

To make sure that Louisbourg would no longer threaten Britain's colonies, Prime Minister William Pitt ordered the systematic destruction of its fortifications. British sappers and miners toiled through the summer of 1760, laying the charges that would seal Louisbourg's fate. The once-flourishing seaport and fortified town would become a modern Carthage. Never again would stone ramparts or ornamental fleur-de-lis line the shores of Louisbourg harbor.

For two hundred years the remains of Louisbourg served as a reminder of the demise of New France. The town lay in ruins, a romantic site that drew few visitors. For those who did come, Louisbourg evoked feelings of melancholy. The comments of the great nineteenth-century American historian Francis Parkman were typical:

> This grassy solitude was once the "Dunkirk of America"; the vaulted caverns where the sheep find shelter from the rain were casemates where terrified women sought refuge from the storms of shot and shell, and the shapeless green mounds were citadel, bastion, rampart and glacis. Here stood Louisbourg; and not all the efforts of its conquerors, nor all the havoc of succeeding times, have availed to efface it.... The remains of its vast defences still tell their tale of human valor and human woe.

Louisbourg, historic Louisbourg, had ceased to exist. Then, as it often does, the unexpected happened. Time made a mockery of the British decision to destroy the French fortress.

Two centuries is a long time, especially in the world of ideas. One concept that developed gradually was heritage protection. Louisbourg received its first commemorative monument in 1895, when an *American* organization raised a memorial to the New England siege of 1745. Canadian appreciation of the fortress's significance was slower to germinate. In 1928 the federal government finally declared Louisbourg an official national historic site; in 1940, a national historic park.

The major turning point came in 1960. At that time the political and economic climate of Canada was right for a visionary proposal dealing with the ruins and rubble of Louisbourg. The combination of a heightened public interest in heritage matters, a federal government sympathetic to nation building, and an increasingly desperate unemployment problem in Cape Breton led to the suggestion that a portion of the fortress be reconstructed. I. C. Rand, a royal commissioner examining the situation of out-of-work Cape Breton coal miners in particular, and the plight of the Canadian coal industry in general, recommended that men be employed re-creating Louisbourg. He concluded that what Cape Breton needed was a "symbolic reconstruction" of its once-glorious fortified town. Such a project, he argued, would not only put hundreds of miners back to work in the short term but would also attract thousands of tourists in the long term. Perhaps surprisingly—after all, how often do governments adopt imaginative solutions?—federal authorities welcomed Rand's proposal. In June 1961 John Diefenbaker's Conservative government announced the decision to reconstruct long-vanished Louisbourg.

On exploring today's re-created eighteenth-century houses and yards, as well as the fortifications, streetscapes, and waterfront, one is transported into another world. The verisimilitude of the past is convincing. Yet there are two ironics worth keeping in mind. First, it was sappers and miners who methodically demolished the fortress in 1760, and it was

IN 1758, BRITAIN LAUNCHED ANOTHER ASSAULT on Louisbourg. It was a contest of epic proportions: twenty-seven thousand British sailors and soldiers blockaded and bombarded the town. Louisbourg fell a second time.

RESEARCHERS LOCATED MORE THAN 500 *maps and plans, such as the 1742 "Plan de la Ville de Louisbourg dans Lisle Royalle."*

miners who were instrumental in its reconstruction two hundred years later. Second, it was the relative completeness of Louisbourg's destruction and abandonment in the 1760s that eventually allowed the town to live again. Had the site been continuously occupied and developed throughout the nineteenth and twentieth centuries—as with Montréal and Québec City, Boston and New York—the archaeological time capsule that was historic Louisbourg would have been lost forever. In that way, Louisbourg was fortunate to have been the only major colonial town not to have had a modern city built on it.

The transformation of eighteenth-century ruins into twentieth-century replicas was not easily achieved. It required a massive effort unprecedented in the Canadian-heritage field. Louisbourg had not been a mere fort or an enclave of a handful of buildings. It had been an entirely fortified town, a *ville fortifiée*, that in its day covered about sixty acres and included hundreds of buildings. Theoretically the whole site could have been reconstructed—it was a question of time, effort, and money. Then again, the approach could have been extremely selective, with only a couple of houses or fortification features rebuilt, enough to give an impression of what had once existed. In the end, though, the winning strategy called for the entire reconstruction of a section of the original town. Under the direction of the federal department responsible for national parks and historic sites, between one fifth and one quarter of Louisbourg was rebuilt: 2 of 7 bastions, more than half a mile of fortifications, 16 of 60 acres within the walls, and 50 of 180 buildings. The challenge of such a monumental undertaking was enormous. Luckily the will to complete the project was not lacking.

The real work of rebuilding Louisbourg did not begin with picks and shovels, backhoes and bulldozers. It began quietly, studiously, in libraries and archives. The original French inhabitants and their New England and British captors had left substantial historical records. Rich treasure-troves of information on Louisbourg and on the French regime in Cape Breton existed in archives in France, Great Britain, and Canada. Fortress researchers located more than 500 relevant maps and plans and approximately 750,000 pages of court, parish, and shipping records, property transactions, siege journals, and much more. The amount of data was, to say the least, daunting.

To make sense of so much eighteenth-century material—documentary, pictorial, and archaeological—the approach was of necessity an interdisciplinary one. For two decades teams of archaeologists, historians, engineers, and architects worked together to sort out the evidence, building by building, street by street. There were large interpretive questions to be asked and to be answered, and there were niggling nuts-and-bolts problems. There were also, inevitably, obstacles. Sometimes the original French plans and documents contradicted themselves. Sometimes archaeological findings did not dovetail with documentary evidence. Sometimes the specific evidence was just not there. (Ruins do not always tell you everything you want to know about roofs and dormers.) And sometimes, of course, one discipline could not understand the point of view of another, leading to innumerable arguments. As one former participant said, "At times there was a lot more heat than light generated in the team meetings." Still, solutions had to be found, and those solutions had to stay within an overall budget.

Construction got under way in 1963. More

than 150 coal miners were hired as laborers, stonemasons, and carpenters to carry out the task of reconstructing more than fifty buildings: the great residences of the engineer and the financial administrator, the comfortable homes of the merchants and the military officers, and the simpler dwellings and the warehouses of the *petit peuple*. All the structures, with one exception, were erected on the foundations of their eighteenth-century predecessors. That exception was the fisherman's house. Today's sea level, a metre higher than it was 250 years ago, prevented archaeologists from finding the ruins of the original home. In all the buildings, however, the eighteenth-century fabric—a cobbled floor here, a part of a wall there—was incorporated wherever possible.

Inside the buildings was another story, one that revolved around their furnishings. More than eight thousand pieces were acquired, including everything from tapestries and paintings to wardrobes and desks, from a harpsichord to china and glass. Some were antiques purchased in France and Québec during the 1960s and 1970s; others were reproductions.

The focus of reconstruction was on the mid-1740s. The town was re-created as it was thought to have looked in the spring of 1745, on the eve of its first siege, or at the apogee of its peacetime development. When devising an animation program, however, park researchers realized that it would be impossible to present all the tumultuous events of 1745. Because they still wanted to provide visitors with a "moment in time," they chose the eventful summer of 1744. In that way, Louisbourg would offer all the drama of France and Britain at war without the damage and destruction of 1745.

The reconstruction of Louisbourg was completed in 1982, and in the end the twenty-two-year undertaking cost approximately $26 million. That may seem like a vast sum, but it was not much for what Louisbourg became: an internationally known tourist destination. In addition, the federal government accomplished its goal of providing employment in Cape Breton. Not only coal miners acquired jobs but also unskilled laborers, artisans, and university students. Many of these people have gained skills as interpreters; local children, too, have learned drumming, fencing, dancing, lacemaking, gardening, hearthside cooking, and public relations.

Louisbourg has been judged a success. Historians, museologists, and tourists alike have given the reborn fortress high marks. For journalists the site has inspired hyperbole: "the jewel in the crown of Canada's historic park system" and "the most ambitious outdoor museum in the country." It has also been called "the best-kept secret in Canada." Unfortunately the fortress is nowhere near as well known as it should be. People still arrive expecting a simple palisade, little realizing that they are about to enter an all-encompassing fortified town.

For today's visitor Louisbourg offers a style of interpretation known as living history. Each year, from June to September, its streets and houses hum with the activities of the original community, as re-created by up to one hundred staff in period costume. Sentries stand guard, drummers lead contingents, bakers make bread, servants cook and clean, smithies work the forge, fishermen clean cod, clerks keep records, gentlemen and ladies do the minuet, mariner-musicians give impromptu concerts, and

innkeepers open their doors to thousands of tourists. The many activities take place indoors and out, both up in the "bastion," where the soldiers are based, and in the "town," where the civilians' lives unfold. Which event or encounter strikes one's fancy depends on one's interests. It may be the wench gossiping in the tavern or the peasants dancing along the quay. It may be the artillery salutes, the fish-cutting demonstrations, or the quiet moment in the chapel.

Architecturally the fortress offers a colonial variant on eighteenth-century French vernacular. The homes and storehouses are all characteristically French, with distinctive shutters and dormers, flared roofs, and ornamental fleur-de-lis. Indeed, some of the buildings look as if they might have been lifted right out of Brittany or Normandy (not surprising given that many of the original inhabitants came from those regions).

Although the town's architecture is not grand (Louisbourg was not Paris, or even Bordeaux), the King's Bastion barracks are a visual highlight. The barracks have an elegant spire, near symmetry, and a black-slate roof that shines in the midday sun. In its original incarnation the structure was one of the largest buildings in North America, containing the Governor's apartment, officers' quarters, a chapel, a prison, and bunkrooms for more than five hundred soldiers. These features have all been re-created, though only a couple of soldiers' rooms were furnished as such. The building also houses modern exhibits. One tells the story of how the fortress was rebuilt; another consists of displays of artifacts excavated by archaeologists. Sundry other modern exhibits, on a variety of themes, are scattered throughout the fortress.

In savoring the texture of this resurrected fortress town, one cannot help but be struck by its overall feel. The fortress has an essence that sets it apart, an elemental quality that suggests timelessness. Perhaps it arises from Louisbourg's solitary setting, perched on the edge of a continent, beneath a perpetually shifting sky, forever facing winds that have blown in off the waters since time began. Or maybe it is the mists and the fogs that never seem far away. Or the glow off buildings in the dying light of late afternoon. The texture of cobbles underfoot. The scent of herbs in the garden, woodsmoke in the kitchen, black powder on the ramparts, and rope and tar in the warehouses. Whatever the source of Louisbourg's distinctive feeling, it leaves a permanent impression, one of exceptional mood and moment, of a time and place that is a link with Canada's past.

LOUISBOURG
THE PHOENIX FORTRESS

SEAPORT

BEFORE IT WAS anything else, Louisbourg was a seaport. A sheltered anchorage, a safe haven, a port of call. Thanks to its spacious and protected harbor, it became a base for fishing vessels, merchant ships, and men-of-war.

Following the French settlement of the town in 1713, Louisbourg quickly emerged as one of the cod-fishing centres in the New World. Hundreds of fishermen, mostly Normans, Bretons, and Basques, made the island port their "home away from home." Cod, drying on the endless rows of flakes, lined the shore outside the walls of the town. The fishing industry not only gave Louisbourg a distinctive scent, it also brought it prosperity.

While the export of dried cod was the kingpin of Louisbourg's economy, merchant trade was also important. The town's harbor, wharves, and quay were always busy with men carrying goods this way and that, into and out of warehouses of wood and stone. When the day's work was done and all the bales and barrels and bundles safely stowed away, it was time to relax. Waterfront inns and cabarets, needless to say, did a booming business.

Louisbourg was one of the New World's busiest ports. Counted among its citizens were hydrographers, pilots, and navigators. Along its shores stood huge storehouses, a careening facility, and Canada's first lighthouse. It is fair to say that Louisbourg's destiny was determined by the sea, for over its waters, carried on the winds of chance, came the fleets of destruction.

THE SEA IS A MAJOR HIGHWAY IN THE *eighteenth century, and for ships from France the road often leads to Louisbourg. Ile Royale is the closest French landfall for ships sailing west. Finding it is fairly easy, for Louisbourg lies on roughly the same latitude as La Rochelle and Rochefort, France's main ports for trading with its colonies. Virtually everyone who comes to Louisbourg arrives by water. Fishermen, merchants, servants, soldiers, and others—they all come and go by boat or ship. The Atlantic crossing, often wild and windy, is the only route they know.*

HOUSES DOT THE LOUISBOURG SHORELINE, *a sign of the town's flourishing fishery and merchant trade. Louisbourg's fishing population comes from two main areas: the Basque-speaking southwest coast of France and the Norman-Breton shoreline near St. Malo. Working inshore and off, in two distinct fishing seasons, the men harvest millions of "finny fellows." The three-man shallop is the most common vessel in the colony, the vessel of choice in the inshore fishery. With masts raised and sails hoisted, fishermen head out along the coast and up to a league offshore in quest of a good day's catch. Returning to port in the evening, they unload their cod, and the processing begins.*

IN AN ERA WITHOUT FREEZING OR CANNING *or rapid transportation, foodstuffs that can withstand long journeys and still have nutritional value are highly prized—dried cod, for example. At the fishing properties that ring Louisbourg harbor the catch is cleaned and processed. Once in someone's kitchen, the dried cod is used in dozens of recipes.*

FOR A MERCHANT A WAREHOUSE CAN BE A *wonderful sight. If the roof is tight and the windows and the doors secure, he knows his goods are at least halfway safe. When his merchandise is protected from theft and spoilage, he can concentrate on what he does best: selling and trading, dickering and dealing. While profit and loss rule the world of merchants, the royal officials in charge of the King's Storehouse (Magazin Général) have other worries. Jean-Baptiste Morin stands at the entrance to Louisbourg's greatest warehouse, wondering whether there will be enough provisions to get the town through the coming winter.*

EACH BOX, EACH BALE, EACH BUNDLE, MUST BE *marked, indicating ownership, destination, and size of shipment. Goods for the King and his overseas colonies carry a fleur-de-lis; "IR" stands for Ile Royale. Merchants have their own range of symbols and abbreviations. This makes life easier for clerk Pierre Lemoule, who must keep track of the comings and goings of goods.*

INSIDE AND OUTSIDE THE MAGAZIN GENERAL, *laborers take a break from their toil. It is a good day's pay lifting bales and barrels for the King, but a man can only move so many before it is time to take a rest. Work starts early and runs late. The work has to get done—there is no doubt about that—but eighteenth-century days are not dominated by a clock.*

WHAT ARE WATERFRONTS IN SEAPORTS FOR, *if not for drinking establishments? Louisbourg's quay offers many choices, and the signs help thirsty customers make up their minds. Indeed, in a world where many cannot read, the artwork, not the words, is what matters. But one Louisbourg cabaret or tavern is not much different from the next. All feature rum and wine, the town's most popular drinks. The rum comes from the Caribbean; the wine, from France.*

LOUISBOURG HAS ITS SHARE OF INNS AS WELL. *There is one price for staying the night, another when lodging includes food. The inn may be clean—the servants do their best—and you may even get a room to yourself. But do not expect it. More than likely you will bed down on a straw mattress the* aubergiste *unrolls after the evening meal is done and the tables are pushed back.*

THERE ARE MORNINGS WHEN THE HARBOR IS *quiet, when there is warmth in the air, and the soft glow of a new day makes it seem as if a mariner's lot is an easy one. But just ask Jacques Germain. His fisherman's face tells a different tale. There is no risk, no danger, he has not seen. Lulls and storms. Wind and spray. The rise and fall of an endless sea. This is the life he knows. Why, last fall two of his crewmates were swept away when a sudden gust turned over their boat. It might have been him. Since that day there is nothing Jacques likes more than to see the great Frédéric Gate take shape along the horizon. It means that once more he has made it safely back to port.*

FORTRESS

LOUISBOURG HAS BEEN CALLED many things: a "modern Carthage," the "Dunkirk of the New World," and the "Gibraltar of North America." What these names mean is that the fortress has been a battleground. Not one but two wars swept over its ramparts and carried its defenders to defeat and exile. Stronghold that it was, Louisbourg was never strong enough to know victory.

In the first half of the eighteenth century the walls of Louisbourg loomed high despite the damp and foggy coast. What were European-style fortifications doing there? But yes, of course, it was La France *outre-mer*. The walls, and the men who fought on them, proclaimed the might of the Monarch, His Most Christian Majesty, His Most Serene Highness, Louis XV, King of France and Navarre. Mere words? Mere titles?

No one dared say that to the men who defended the kingdom.

Louisbourg's soldiers were a mixed lot, a mix found in any army: officers and enlisted men, old and young, brave and cowardly. On the eve of the 1745 siege by New England colonists, three quarters of the soldiers—560 in all—were marine troops (*compagnies franches de la marine*) recruited in France to fight in the colonies overseas. The other quarter comprised a contingent of Swiss and German mercenaries, mostly Protestant, and an elite group of artillery specialists. By the outbreak of the British siege in 1758 Louisbourg's garrison had grown more than sixfold. The marines and cannoneers were still there, in greater numbers, but now there were "professional" soldiers as well: battalions from four of France's land-army regiments. In the end, despite the skill and strength of its forces, Louisbourg was overthrown again.

THE BEAT OF THE DRUMS IS A CONSTANT *reminder that Louisbourg is a fortified stronghold. Drum rolls, heard every few hours, set the pace of the town. They announce the opening of the gates in the morning, the closing of the gates at night. They also accompany various military manoeuvres throughout the day.*

LOUISBOURG, LIKE ALL FORTIFIED TOWNS OF *the eighteenth century, is a work of geometry. Its pentagonal bastions are linked by straight-line curtain walls, and its precise side-by-side gun embrasures flank each of those bastions. The bastions themselves are located where they must be, on whatever high land is available (not very high in Louisbourg's case). It is textbook fortification design, seen over and over again at hundreds of European fortresses. A man like François Richer is responsible for putting so much architectural theory into practice. His skills as a stonecutter have helped transform sandstone, limestone, and rubblestone into a stronghold.*

LOUISBOURG'S HIGH STONE REVETMENTS, *along with the marshy terrain that fronts the defences, are considered sufficient to keep the British at bay on the fortress's landward side. Alas, the best-laid plans of military engineers do go awry on occasion. Fine walls are never enough, not by a long shot. In 1745 and in 1758 British armies will advance on this front. It will take weeks of bombardment, but finally the enemy cannons and mortars will succeed.*

EVERY ERA HAS SYMBOLS, AND DURING THE *eighteenth-century world of Louisbourg the dominant symbol is that of the King. Gates and bastions, for example, are named after members of the royal family. As you enter the town on the landward side, passing through the Dauphin Gate, a bright-white limestone carving shines down. It is the coat of arms of the King, Louis XV. Another common symbol is found on the blue-coated soldiers. The anchor insignia on their cartridge cases reveals that they are in the pay of the Ministry of the Marine.*

WITHOUT ENOUGH SOLDIERS—TRAINED TO *handle muskets and cannons and to stand and face enemy fire—no fortress can be protected. Louisbourg's defenders are more accustomed to constructing fortifications than to fighting on them. Nonetheless, they do their best. It will not suffice, however. In both sieges they are outnumbered and outflanked.*

COLLECTIVELY, THE SOLDIERS OF A TOWN ARE *known as its garrison. Individually, they are known by* noms de guerre—*each soldier has a colorful* sobriquet, *or nickname. Some names inspire military confidence: La Guerre (War) and Sans Peur (Without Fear). Others evoke images of a garden: La Fleur, La Rose, and La Violette. Still others suggest merriment and light-heartedness: Belle Humeur (Good Mood), Bon Appétit (Good Appetite), Prêt à Boire (Ready to Drink), Sans Souci (Without a Care), and Sans Regret (Without Regret).*

A SOLDIER OFTEN SAYS THAT HIS BEST FRIEND *is his musket. That may seem like an exaggeration to a civilian, but a soldier's life may one day depend on whether his musket fires straight and true. Therefore he cares for his weapon the way a fisherman cares for his boat. Similarly, a soldier wants to be ready for war. The drills in the court-yard of the bastion are tedious, but the men complain only for effect.*

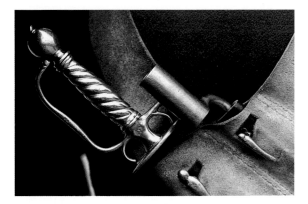

MOVE AND MUSCLE, SWAB AND CHARGE, RAM *and ready. The cannoneers do their job. Dressed in bright red, the artillery specialists operate the cannons, unleashing their flash of light, their sudden thunder. Louisbourg has only thirty such cannoneers to more than one hundred cannons. They are an elite group and are not shy about letting the "ordinary" soldiers know it. When the soldiers mutiny on the day after Christmas, 1744, the artillerymen have no part of it. They side with the officers. "Vive le Roi!"*

WHILE ONE WANTS MEN TO DEFEND A FORTRESS, *one often has to settle for boys. More than a few of Louisbourg's soldiers are still in their teens, some even younger than the official minimum age, sixteen. Age aside, officers do require their recruits to be patriotic. Such sentiments do not run deep in the eighteenth century. Desertions are common, and routine garrison infractions—drunkenness, disorderly conduct, and uncleanliness—are even more prevalent.*

SMALL BOYS HAVE DREAMED OF BEING SOLDIERS *for as long as there have been armies. Some like to hide in and around the wooden* guérite, *a lookout that juts out over the harbor not far from the guardpost of the Dauphin Demi-Bastion. Others ponder what they would do with real swords. In Louisbourg, bristling with hundreds of soldiers, boys watch the men stand guard and march and drill. Unfortunately for the lads, not one will ever join the troops, not one will ever be able to trade his boyish buckles for a swordbelt—at least not for as long as he lives on Ile Royale. The King wants the colonial population to grow and prosper, so he has forbidden the recruiting of soldiers from within New France. All the men of the garrison come from the mother country.*

THE WORD "AESTHETICS" DOES NOT USUALLY *come to mind when one speaks of fortresses. Yet many aspects of Louisbourg were graceful and elegant. Thanks to its military engineers—professionals trained not only in building techniques but also in classical architecture—Louisbourg has a look that is at once simple and refined. From the cobblestone passages that charm passersby to the vistas that reward a hundred vantage points, Louisbourg is a visual feast.*

COMMUNITY

EVERY COMMUNITY IS distinctive, though few more so than Louisbourg. Here was a town, a major centre in New France, for which neither a fur trade nor a seigniorial regime held any importance. Instead, its orientation was almost entirely toward the sea. Its heroes were merchants and mariners, not explorers and *coureurs de bois*. Here, too, was a settlement, overwhelmingly French and Catholic, where the parishioners did not pay tithes or make contributions to a church. They preferred to save their money and to attend the garrison chapel, paid for by the King. Yes, Louisbourg was a parsimonious community.

It was also very much a man's town. One expects that in a busy seaport and military stronghold, but in Louisbourg the numbers were especially surprising. Men sometimes outnumbered women by as much as ten to one; even at the best of times the ratio was at least three to one. These were good odds for a young woman looking for a husband, but they were not so good for a young man seeking a bride.

Nonetheless, Louisbourg was home to many families. In 1713, men, women, and children relocated there from Placentia, Newfoundland. In the years that followed, new emigrants—seamstresses from Brittany, stonemasons from Normandy, butchers from Paris, and navigators from Québec—helped the seaport town grow and prosper. They raised their families in a range of dwellings. The simplest were vertical-log structures. Then there were more substantial timber-frame homes. Finally, there were ever-impressive masonry residences. Whatever the house, the goals of the families were the same: to make a decent living and to give their children a good start in life.

IN LOUISBOURG A LOT OF AMUSEMENTS TAKE *place in the street. In fact, townspeople take advantage of any open space. Nine-pin, for example, is a popular pastime for both children and adults.*

THE CLOCK ON THE KING'S BASTION BARRACKS *has only one arm. One can see the hour, even the half-hour, at a glance, and that is usually enough in the eighteenth century. It is not yet a world of hurry and go, seconds and split seconds. Pocketwatches and wall clocks exist but are not yet found in every home. Indeed, for most people, the clock on the barracks, with its ringing chimes, is accurate enough for a pace of life satisfied with hourglasses and garden sundials.*

THE GREENS OF THE GARDENS GIVE COLOR TO *an otherwise grey world. Hardly a house in Louisbourg does not take advantage of its yard. Many yards are given over entirely to gardens of herbs and vegetables. Sitting in raised beds, protected by fences from chilly sea breezes, the plantings are pleasing to both sight and smell. Symmetry is essential. So is the placement of fragrant plants close to pathways, where passers-by can enjoy them most.*

THE STREETS OF LOUISBOURG RUN NORTH AND *south, east and west, one of the advantages of a town started from scratch. Military engineers have laid a grid that residents must observe. A local regulation stipulates that the front of buildings must be right on the street. It makes for excellent viewing of the world passing by one's door. Religious processions, public displays of justice, goods in transit, dances, mothers and children—all color the streets of Louisbourg.*

"UPPER," "MIDDLE," AND "LOWER" ARE THE *terms used to describe the classes of society. In truth, however, it is far more complicated than that. There are classes within classes, and pecking orders within pecking orders. Each individual, each group, tries to find a means to rise above his rivals. Servants compare masters and tasks; merchants such as Monsieur Castaing show off their success by the way they dress. The* gens de qualité *exhibit a casual grace that comes easily to people born to wealth and leisure.*

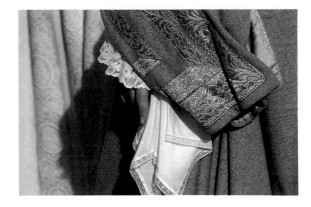

SMALL DETAILS SOMETIMES TELL LARGE TALES. *The grace of an exit, the poise of a promenade, the turn of a calf—these are some of the ways people of leisure strive to show their breeding. When they fear that style is not enough, they wear or carry items that symbolize their status. Their jewellery and canes, their lace and trim, speak of birth and wealth. Louisbourg is not Versailles, but it has its share of nobility. And pretension.*

LOUISBOURG'S TOWNSPEOPLE ARE SO *parsimonious that they prefer to worship in the garrison chapel, the Chapelle Saint-Louis, rather than build a proper church at their own expense. They also prefer to see their parish served by Récollets (members of a branch of the Franciscan Order), not secular priests. The Récollets, including Father Isidore Caulet, are on the King's payroll—one less expense for the parishioners. The statue of Saint-Roch is in the chapel, as is the miniature ship, a votive offering to God from mariners whose lives have been spared in a storm at sea.*

PRETTY MARGUERITE AND LIVELY THERESE *look forward to the day when they can marry. It is a day that comes sooner in Louisbourg than in France or even in Québec. Men greatly out-number women in Louisbourg, so girls usually find themselves at the altar while still in their teens. In fact, in the eyes of church and state, twelve is the minimum age for a girl to marry, provided of course that her parents give consent. Girls require their parents' consent until they turn twenty-five; boys cannot marry before age fourteen and must seek permission until they reach age thirty.*

A FRIEND TO CHATTER WITH OR A GAME OF *roll in the grass or seesaw is usually more than enough to put a smile on any child's face. But childhood does not last long in the eighteenth century. Some boys and girls find themselves working as servants by age seven; many others begin learning a trade by age twelve. Only the children of the well-to-do ever master the skills of reading and writing.*

ANIMALS ARE KEPT FOR ONE REASON ONLY: *their usefulness. Sheep supply wool; goats, milk; hens, geese, and ducks, eggs. All, eventually, supply meat. Even then, Louisbourg inhabitants do not raise nearly enough livestock to feed themselves. Hundreds of cattle and sheep have to be purchased from farmers in Acadia, and other food supplies are imported from France, New England, and the French settlements along the St. Lawrence River. That does not mean that animals are not a common sight. Sheep, for example, can be found grazing along the walls of the town; pigs can be seen in pens (a law prohibits them from roaming free).*

THE SHAPE OF THE PAST IS NOT ALWAYS WHAT *one expects. The sharply angled cone is not something dreamed up by a carpenter playing with geometry. It is a glacière, or an icehouse, the closest thing in the eighteenth century to a deepfreeze. The door to the icehouse is on the north side. Inside, one finds a deep well, which in winter is filled with ice that is used to keep meat and other perishables for extended periods; the Governor also has ice to cool his wine in summer. The fleur-de-lis on the peak of the icehouse adorns many public buildings.*

THE KITCHEN IS THE HEART OF THE TYPICAL *eighteenth-century house. Each one is different yet the same. Pots and pans, crocks and ladles, skimmers and measures, and chopping blocks stand at the ready. The cooks know a hundred recipes, most of which they learned at their mother's knee. A pinch of this and a dash of that is as exacting as they need to be. They can tell when a dish is done by merely tasting, looking, and smelling. With much of the meat and fish preserved through salting and drying, the appreciated cooks are the ones who can add just the right sauce.*

THE ROOFS OF THE TOWN HAVE THEIR OWN *stories to tell, for each reflects its owner. Some owners can afford the best shingles; others make do with second best. But only the King—on government buildings—can pay for shining black slate. Roofs also speak of line and angle, texture and surface. In Louisbourg the roofs are steep, making it easy to shed rain and snow. Rooftop ladders allow owners easy access to chimneys, to clean flues before the risk of smoke and flames.*

IF LOUISBOURG IS A WINDOW ON THE PAST, *then what do its windows reveal? Why, that depends. Some show soldiers lingering in the barracks, away from the call of a sergeant's voice or the scrutiny of a lieutenant's eye. Others show the craftsmanship that provides protection from wind, cold, and theft. Meanwhile, in a tavern window opening onto the waterfront, weary Suzanne gazes dreamily at the sea.*

THE EIGHTEENTH-CENTURY WORLD IS RULED *largely by the rising and setting of the sun. Windows, therefore, are important: where they are located, how large they are, and how much light they let in. It does not matter whether it is the Governor's bedroom in the King's Bastion barracks or a simply furnished room in a small house. Sunlight is the major source of illumination. Candles, lamps, and fireplaces do provide a night-time glow, but most work is accomplished in daylight.*

THERE IS TIME FOR REFLECTION IN THIS NEW *World town. Servanne, a Breton girl, composes her thoughts outside her place of work. Another hour, just one more hour, she says to herself, and her day will be done. André, a scrivener who toils with a quill, stops to wonder what brought him to Louisbourg. Fine clerk that he is, he vows to return to France someday, to make his mark. And Joannis, the hefty Basque who lifts and carries for the merchant Monsieur Rodrigue, must pause to rest his weary arms. Soon he will be back in Bayonne, France, with his wife and family.*